A Game of Shapes

Christine Lindop

Name _____

Age _____

Class _____

OXFORD
UNIVERSITY PRESS

Reading Dolphins
Notes for teachers & parents

📖 Using the book

1 Begin by looking at the first picture (page 2). Look at the picture and ask questions about it. Then read the text and the question under the picture with your students. Give them time to answer the question. Then, together, read the answer at the top of the next page. **Use section 1 of the CD for this if possible.**

2 Teach and check the understanding of any new vocabulary. Note that some of the words are in the **Picture Dictionary** on pages 16–17.

3 Now look at the activities below the answer (page 3). Show the example to the students and instruct them to complete the activities. This may be done individually, in pairs, or as a class.

4 Do the same for the remaining pages of the book.

5 Retell the whole story more quickly, reinforcing the new vocabulary. **Sections 2 and 3 of the CD can help with this.**

6 **If possible, listen to the expanded story (section 4 of the CD). The students should follow in their books.**

7 Use the **Picture Dictionary** to check that students understand and remember new vocabulary. **Section 5 of the CD can help with this.**

💿 Using the CD

The CD contains five sections.

1 The story told slowly, with pauses. Use this during the first reading. It may also be used for "Listen and repeat" activities at any point.

2 The story told at normal speed. This should be used once the students have read the book for the first time.

3 The story chanted. Students may want to chant along with the story.

4 The expanded story. The story is told in a longer version. This will help the students understand English when it is spoken faster, as they will now know the story and the vocabulary.

5 Vocabulary. Each word in the **Picture Dictionary** is spoken and then used in a simple sentence.

It is red.

It is a circle.

What is it?

★ Answer on page 3

2

*It is a ball.

Connect.

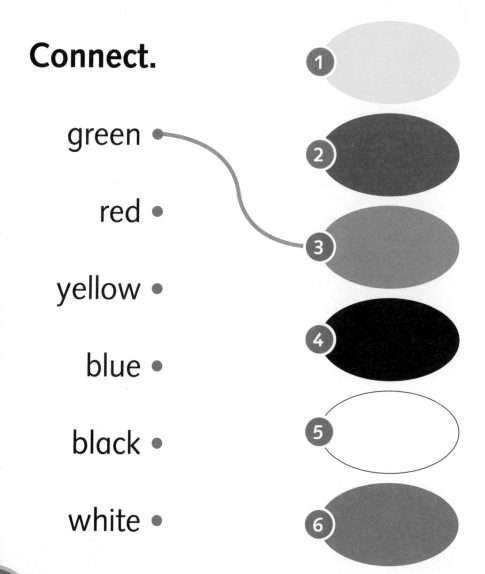

green

red

yellow

blue

black

white

1

2

3

4

5

6

3

It is blue.

It is a square.

What is it?

★ Answer on page 5

4

*It is a box.

Number.

ball 3 pen ☐   bed ☐

cup ☐   box ☐   book ☐

It is brown.
It is a triangle.
What is it?

★ Answer on page 7

6

*It is a sandwich.

How many?

❶ I can see ⬜ 5 ⬜ ovals.

❷ I can see ⬜ triangles.

❸ I can see ⬜ squares.

❹ I can see ⬜ circles.

❺ I can see ⬜ diamonds.

It is green.

It is a rectangle.

What is it?

★ Answer on page 9

8

*It is a book.

Connect.

a blue circle •　　　　　① 1

a blue oval •　　　　　2

a green diamond •　　　3

a green square •　　　4

a red circle •　　　　5

a red square •　　　　6

9

It is white.

It is an oval.

What is it?

★ Answer on page 11

*It is an egg.

Draw.

two diamonds	four circles
three triangles	two squares

It is yellow.
It is a diamond.
What is it?

★ Answer on page 13

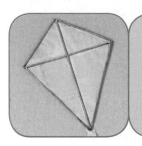

*It is a kite.

Look at the kite.
Circle yes or no .

❶ It is blue.	yes	(no)
❷ It is yellow.	yes	no
❸ It is red.	yes	no
❹ It is a ball.	yes	no
❺ It is a kite.	yes	no
❻ It is a diamond.	yes	no
❼ It is green.	yes	no
❽ It is a circle.	yes	no

It is pink.
It is a heart.
What is it?

★ Answer on page 15

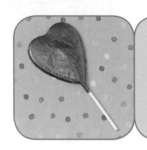

*It is candy.

Look at page 14.
Circle yes or no .

① The heart is pink.
    yes
    no

② The bag is blue.
    yes
    no

③ The apple is green.
    yes
    no

④ The boy has a green shirt.
    yes
    no

⑤ The girl has a pink shirt.
    yes
    no

Picture Dictionary

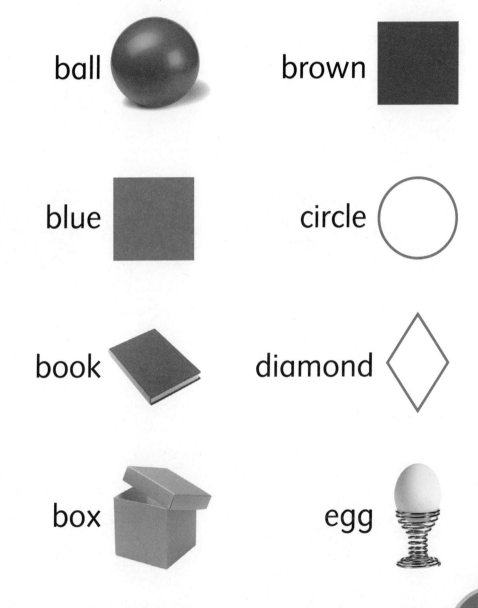

ball

brown

blue

circle

book

diamond

box

egg

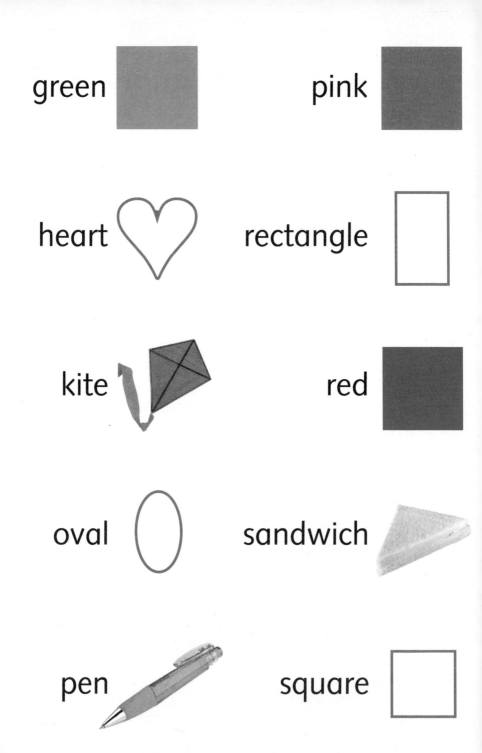

green

pink

heart

rectangle

kite

red

oval

sandwich

pen

square

Dolphin Readers

Dolphin Readers are available at five levels, from Starter to 4.

The Dolphins series covers four major themes:

Grammar, Living Together, The World Around Us, Science and Nature.

For each theme, there are two titles at every level.

Activity Books are available for all Dolphins.

All Dolphins are available on audio CD.
(2 TITLES ON EACH CD ◎ SEE TABLE BELOW)

Teacher's Notes are available at **www.oup.com/elt/dolphins**

	Grammar	Living Together	The World Around Us	Science and Nature
Starter	• Silly Squirrel • Monkeying Around	• My Family • A Day with Baby	• Doctor, Doctor • Moving House	• A Game of Shapes • Baby Animals
Level 1	• Meet Molly • Where Is It?	• Little Helpers • Jack the Hero	• On Safari • Lost Kitten	• Number Magic • How's the Weather?
Level 2	• Double Trouble • Super Sam	• Candy for Breakfast • Lost!	• A Visit to the City • Matt's Mistake	• Numbers, Numbers Everywhere • Circles and Squares
Level 3	• Students in Space • What Did You Do Yesterday?	• New Girl in School • Uncle Jerry's Great Idea	• Just Like Mine • Wonderful Wild Animals	• Things That Fly • Let's Go to the Rainforest
Level 4	• The Tough Task • Yesterday, Today and Tomorrow	• We Won the Cup • Up and Down	• Where People Live • City Girl, Country Boy	• In the Ocean • Go, Gorillas, Go

OXFORD
UNIVERSITY PRESS

Great Clarendon Street, Oxford OX2 6DP

Oxford University Press is a department of the University of Oxford.
It furthers the University's objective of excellence in research, scholarship,
and education by publishing worldwide in

Oxford New York

Auckland Cape Town Dar es Salaam Hong Kong Karachi
Kuala Lumpur Madrid Melbourne Mexico City Nairobi
New Delhi Shanghai Taipei Toronto

With offices in

Argentina Austria Brazil Chile Czech Republic France Greece
Guatemala Hungary Italy Japan South Korea Poland Portugal
Singapore Switzerland Thailand Turkey Ukraine Vietnam

OXFORD and OXFORD ENGLISH are registered trade marks of
Oxford University Press in the UK and in certain other countries

ISBN 9780194400800

Printed in China

Commissioned photography by: Mark Mason
Illustrations by: Mark Ruffle
With thanks to Sally Spray for her contribution to this series